Skyscrapers

by
David C

Ransom

Thunderbolts

Skyscrapers
by David Orme

Illustrated by Dan Chernett

Published by Ransom Publishing Ltd.
Radley House, 8 St. Cross Road, Winchester, Hants. SO23 9HX, UK
www.ransom.co.uk

ISBN 978 178127 069 1

First published in 2013

A CIP catalogue record of this book is available from the British Library.

THUNDER
BOLTS

Contents

Skyscrapers: The Facts

Skyscrapers are not new!

2,500 years old

THUNDER BOLTS

1,400 years old

The Pyramids: 4,500 years old

Tall towers

Bologna towers, Italy (about 1400), 97m high

Washington Monument (1884), 169m high

CN Tower, Toronto
(1976), 553m high
Tokyo Skytree
(2012), 634m high

The first skyscrapers

New York City, 1870

Chicago, 1884

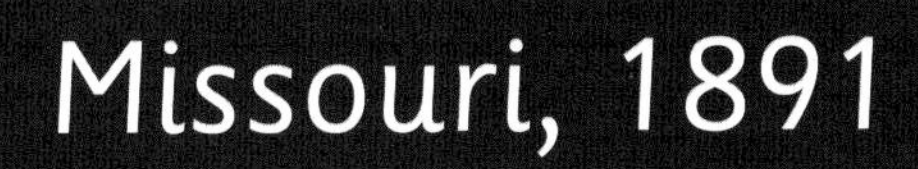
Missouri, 1891

New York,
1903

What you need

Concrete
Steel

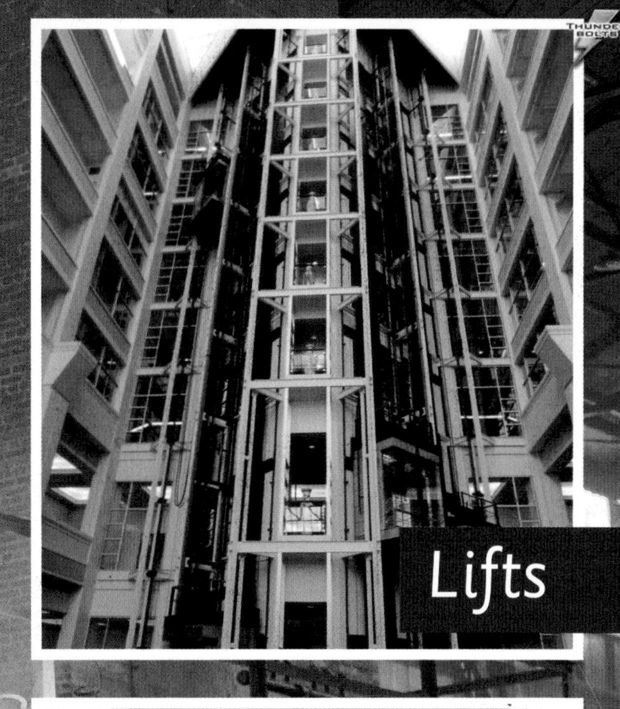
Lifts

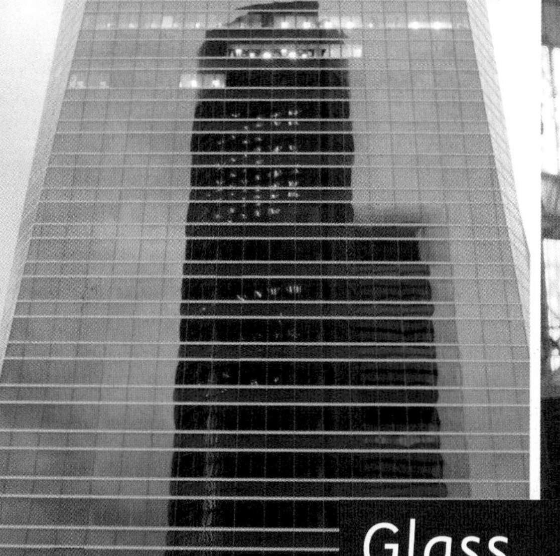
Glass

Skyscrapers and earthquakes

Tokyo, Japan – earthquake zone!

THUNDER BOLTS
Keeping buildings safe.

New York – skyscraper city

Before 11th September 2011 ...

... and after.

What happened?

Climbing skyscrapers

THUNDER BOLTS

Are they crazy?

The world's tallest

1

828m

2

601m

3

509m

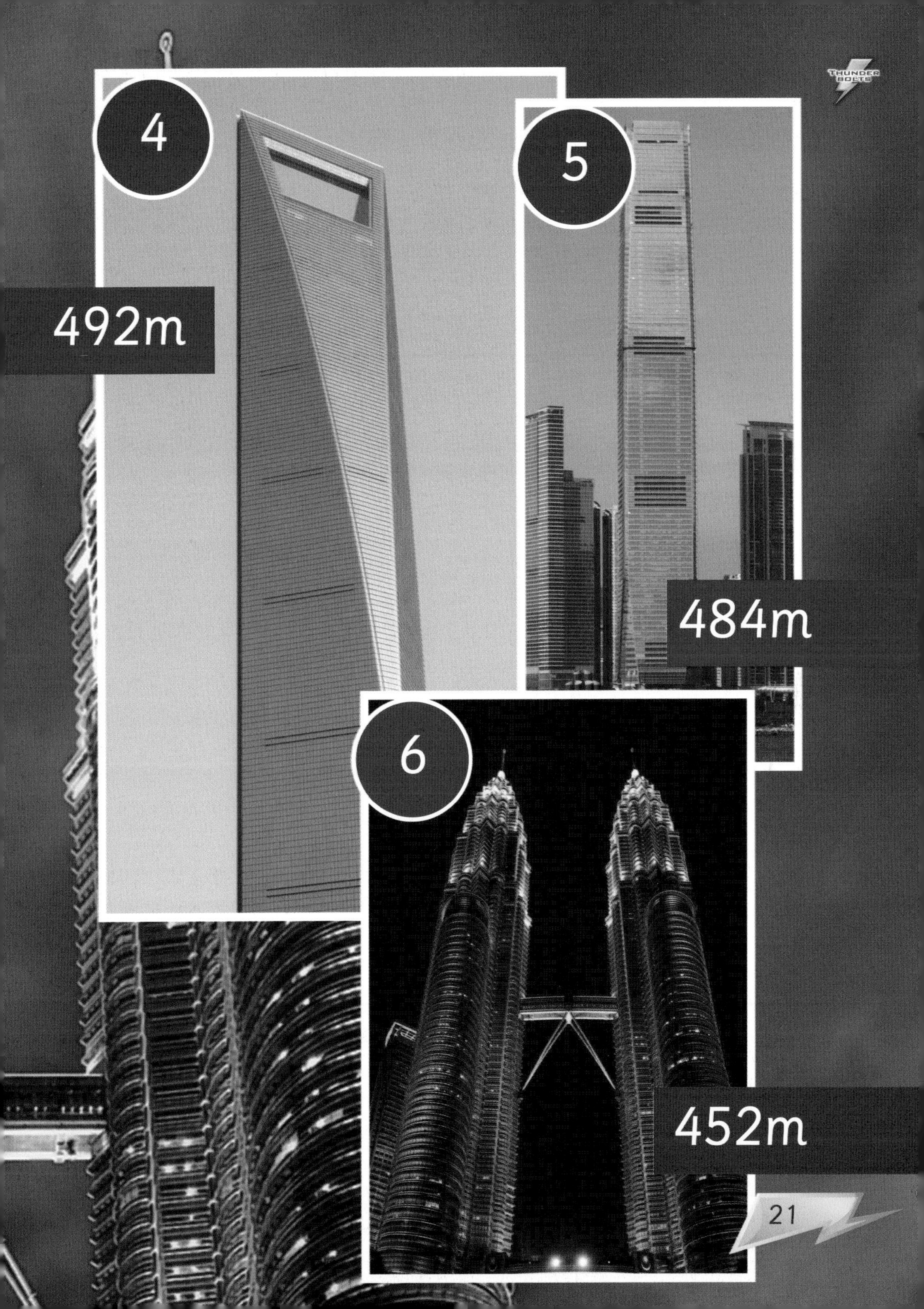
THUNDER BOLTS
4
492m
5
484m
6
452m

THUNDER BOLTS
Future skyscrapers
How high will they be?

I hope it's not out of order!

THUNDER BOLTS

13

Floor 13

Tom has a meeting with Mr Brown.

THUNDER BOLTS
11. Mr. Smit
12. Mr. Brow
14. Mrs. Todd
15. Mr. Gree

What's on floor 13?
12

13

It doesn't look good, Tom!

Just a quick look!
13

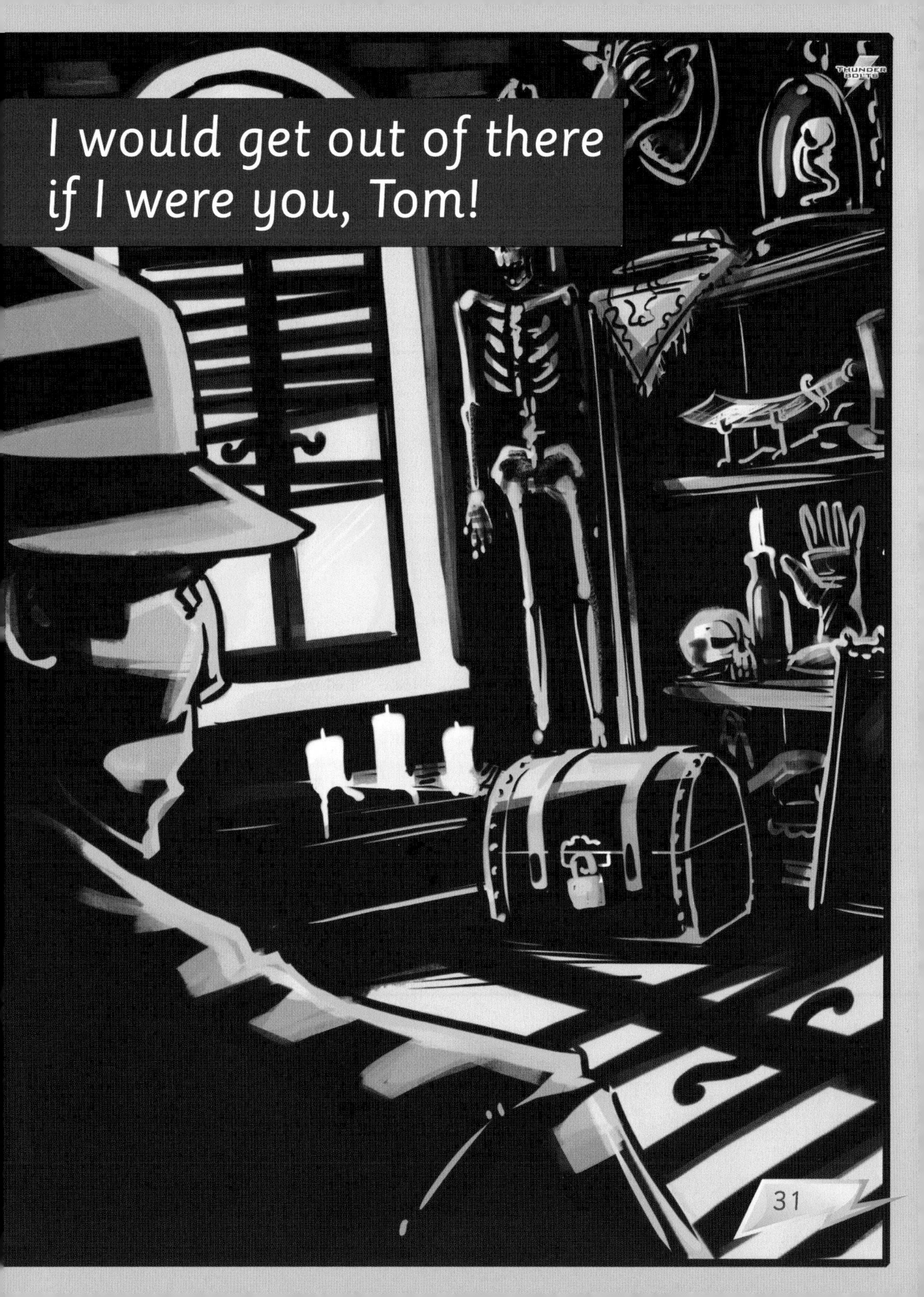
I would get out of there if I were you, Tom!

THUNDER BOLTS
I told you not to go in there!

Is Tom in trouble?

Not really!

That was great acting!

Tom's in the money!

THUNDER BOLTS
FLOOR 13 THE MOVIE
STARRING TOM
NOW SHOWING
FLOOR 13

Word list

building
concrete
earthquake
future
glass
monument
pyramid
skyscraper
steel
tower
trouble
zone